A HOME FOR ALL CHILDREN

GW00731301

The story of Dr Barnardo

The school run by Tom Barnardo in the East End of London was very different from schools as we know them today. For one thing there were only three classes a week—one on Sundays and two on evenings during the week. The lessons were held in a donkey stable. There was just the one room, with a few rows of wooden benches and no desks. A stove in the corner provided the only heating in winter.

It was over a hundred years ago, in 1866, when Barnardo started his first school. In those days, if parents wanted their children to go to a proper school, they had to pay. Mostly only rich people could afford it. The result was that few people were able to read and write, which meant they could never get a good job.

The pupils at Barnardo's school went because they wanted to learn. Every class was full. Sometimes as many as two hundred children and young people crowded into the stable. The youngest pupil was about six years old, and the oldest was even older than the teacher!

The school was known as a "Ragged School". This was because the boys and girls who attended were dressed in rags—they were too poor to afford proper clothing. There

1

were many such schools all over the country. The teachers had no training and were not paid for their work. They just wanted to help the children to learn to read and write. But Barnardo taught his pupils about the Bible as well.

The "Ragged School" – pupils outside the donkey-stable

Barnardo realised, however, that his pupils also needed work. So he took in extra helpers, who taught the boys a trade and the girls to make clothes for themselves. He was later able to find jobs for some of his boys.

When Barnardo first started teaching at his school he found it hard to control the pupils. They tested him with all sorts of tricks. Some of them threw rotten eggs and oranges at him. Once he was pelted with "pepper bombs". But before long Barnardo won the respect and admiration of his pupils. They began to realise that he really cared for them. They stopped their tricks and would allow no one to harm their teacher.

One night, going home after school, Barnardo discovered that six of the roughest boys in his school were following him. He wondered what trouble they were up to. Imagine his relief when he found out they only wanted to protect him! They had heard of a plan to attack him, and formed a bodyguard to make sure that he got back safely.

The young preacher

Tom Barnardo was a twenty-one-year-old student when he started his school in the donkey stable. He was training at the nearby London Hospital to be a doctor. Soon he hoped to go to China as a missionary. Meanwhile, on two evenings a week, he went around the East End preaching.

On one occasion he was leading a meeting on a street corner. A crowd had stopped to listen to him, including some who were obviously out for a bit of fun. After Barnardo had preached, he closed his eyes for a prayer. At that point, a mud pie hit him right in the face, stopping his mouth. The crowd burst into laughter, the guilty lad making a quick get-away.

But this kind of treatment did not put him off. As well as preaching, Barnardo also visited homes and public houses, selling Bibles.

At one pub he found himself in a bar filled with teen-age boys and girls. As soon as he entered, two big fellows jumped up and shut the door behind him. Barnardo sensed trouble and saw there was no way out of it. He decided to put on a brave act and walked to the centre of the room.

"I have come to offer you the Word of God," he told them.

"Chuck 'im out," somebody shouted.

"I will let you have the whole Bible for threepence," the student went on. "Or you can have the New Testament for a penny."

"Let's 'ave the books," yelled another boy.

"Be fair," said Barnardo, jumping on to a table. "These books cost me double the price."

Without letting him say any more, several of the teenagers, the worse for drink, leapt at him. In a moment the table was overturned and poor Barnardo was lying underneath it. He tried to escape, but was too dazed to do so.

When the lads had stopped fooling about, they let the student get up and sent him on his way. Barnardo managed to get back to his rooms only with great difficulty. He had two broken ribs, as well as being badly bruised. It was six weeks before he was better.

Later that evening a policeman called to see him. He urged him to take the gang to court. Barnardo refused. He had offered them the Gospel and did not want to end by having the law on them. In any case, he felt that he was partly to blame for going into the pub in the first place.

The boys who had attacked him were surprised when they heard he would not make a charge against them. They decided that, from then on, nobody would be allowed to harm the young preacher. Every day, until he was better, some of the gang called on Barnardo to see how he was getting on. Afterwards he was able to go about selling his Bibles without any more trouble.

Years later Barnardo said that this event did more than anything to open doors into homes in the East End.

Homeless boys

However, the most important event to occur, showing him where his future lay, came after school one winter's night.

School was over and the children had left. Barnardo was about to close the door and go home when he saw a boy warming himself by the stove.

"Come on, lad, time to go home," the teacher said.

"Please let me stop, sir," asked Jim Jarvis.

"Stop? Why, your mother will wonder what has happened to you."

"I ain't got no mother," replied Jim.

"Well, what about your father?"

"I ain't got no father either."

"Nonsense, lad. Where do you live?"

"Don't live nowhere," explained the boy.

"Well, where did you sleep last night?" went on the teacher.

"Down in Whitechapel, in a cart filled with 'ay."

Barnardo was startled by what he heard. Could it be true that this ten-year-old boy really had no parents? And that he slept out rough?

"Are there any other boys like you, without a home?" asked Barnardo.

"Oh yes, lots of 'em," was the reply.

Surely the boy must be telling a lie, thought Barnardo. But suppose he was telling the truth? He decided to put Jim's story to the test.

"If I give you a meal and a bed for the night, will you show me where these boys sleep?"

Jim Jarvis jumped at the chance. He had never slept in a proper bed before. And so half an hour after midnight, when they had finished their supper, the two of them set out.

They walked the streets of Stepney in search of sleeping children. At first there was no sign of anybody sleeping out on that cold winter's night. Barnardo was beginning to think that Jim must have made it all up. Then the boy led the way down a side passage, which ended in a high wall. Beyond was the roof of an old clothes shop.

"Where now?" asked the teacher, getting a bit angry.

"They're up there," explained Jim, pointing to the roof.

The boy climbed the wall and then pulled his teacher up behind him. And there, on the flat part of the roof, lay

Barnardo and Jim Jarvis searching for homeless children

eleven poorly dressed boys. They were all fast asleep. They were hunched up close to each other, to keep themselves warm. Their ages were from about eight to eighteen years.

"Shall I wake 'em up?" asked Jim.

But Barnardo had seen enough for one night. In his heart he prayed that God might in some way care for these homeless boys. Little did he realise that God would use him in answer to his prayer.

Next day Barnardo arranged for Jim Jarvis to be looked after by a family he knew. Later, when he was old enough, Jim was sent to Canada to start a new life as a farmer.

The East End

In Barnardo's time, most of London's poorest people lived in the East End. The number of people living in the capital was growing rapidly, and many of them were out of work. There was no unemployment benefit or social security in those days, which meant that people without jobs found it almost impossible to live. Those who did have a job received low wages.

Parents often relied upon their children to bring in some money. Children had to do odd jobs, like selling matches or flowers. Many of them were forced to go begging. If they returned home empty-handed, they were beaten. If the children earned no money at all, some parents turned them out and told them to look after themselves. Some parents even sold their children to cruel people who used them for cheap labour.

Housing conditions were terrible. There were rows upon rows of small back-to-back houses. Few of the houses had water or lighting. Some had a toilet in the backyard, but many had to use a bucket. Poor families usually lived in only one room.

To escape from their troubles, many grown-ups and even young people took to drinking. Nearly every street had its own public house. Pubs were open until midnight. It was a common sight to see people drunk at any time of the day. And when they had spent all their money on drink, there was nothing left for things like food and clothing.

Children were often uncared for by their parents. They were dressed in cast-off clothing, and went unwashed and hungry. When they were ill, there was no money for medicine

A homeless boy

or to pay for a doctor. (In those days there was no free health service. You had to pay for everything.)

Hundreds of children died before they reached their teens. Many were driven to commit suicide.

Thousands of children, however, found it better to take to the streets and look after themselves. If they could not earn or beg a few pennies, then they were forced to steal. At one time Barnardo reckoned that there were about 30 000 homeless boys and girls living on the streets of the East End. And on any one night there would be another 15 000 children who had no home but managed to find the money for a bed in a lodging-house.

Lord Shaftesbury

One evening, at a church meeting in North London, the speaker did not turn up. Without warning, Barnardo was called upon to take his place. He took the chance to talk about his school in Stepney. He also told of his meeting with Jim Jarvis and the homeless boys. By the time he had finished, many of his listeners were in tears.

Afterwards a young girl came up to him. She handed him a small packet. "I was going to give this money for missionaries," she explained. "Now I want you to have it for your homeless children."

Barnardo did not quite know what to do. He had never before been given any money for his children's work. But he could not refuse the gift. Perhaps, he thought, this was God's way of showing him what He wanted him to do?

A week later Barnardo received a letter from Lord Shaftesbury, who wanted to hear more about the homeless boys. Barnardo went to Lord Shaftesbury's home, where he met several other important people. After supper Shaftesbury asked about the children.

"Tell me, are these reports about homeless children true?"

"Yes, my lord," answered the student.

"I suppose you know where to find these children?" Shaftesbury went on. "Could you find any of them tonight?"

"Certainly," replied Barnardo. "Any time about midnight. I know of two or three places where they sleep."

So, just after twelve o'clock that night, a small group of men could be seen making their way through Billingsgate Market, near the River Thames. At first it seemed as though the visitors were going to be disappointed. There was no sign of sleeping children.

Then Barnardo noticed a possible hiding-place under a large canvas cover. He drew back the cover and pulled out a thin, poorly dressed lad. Within moments, other boys were found at the same spot.

In the end Barnardo had seventy-three boys lined up for Shaftesbury to see. A few minutes later the boys were being treated to a meal of coffee, hot sausages, and bread and butter at Dick Fisher's Coffee Shop.

Shaftesbury watched the boys gulp down the food. He turned to Barnardo and said, with tears in his eyes, "All London must know about this."

The meal was over by three o'clock in the morning. As Shaftesbury was about to return home, he shook the student by the hand. "God bless and lead you, young man," he said. "Keep up your good work."

Finding God's will

As yet, Barnardo had not thought of opening a home for the street-boys. His next move was to open a mission. This was to be a sort of club where he could hold preaching services and also have classes for children and grown-ups.

A group of Christians who had heard of his work gave

him enough money to buy two old cottages, opposite the donkey stable. He knocked down the inside walls to make a large hall. He called his club the East End Juvenile Mission.

On several days of the week Barnardo held services in the hall. As a result of his preaching many people became Christians. They joined together to start a church, with Barnardo as the minister. He stayed in charge of the People's Church, as it was called, for several years. Then, because

Dr Barnardo as a young man

the crowds became so big, he later bought a public house where he was able to have bigger meetings.

All the time he was doing this work he carried on with his training at the hospital. But he began to wonder if perhaps God was showing him that he should stay in London to care for the children.

He waited and prayed, wanting to be sure what to do. Then one day as he was reading his Bible and thinking about his future, it seemed as though God was speaking to him. He read these words: "The Lord says, I will teach you the way you should go . . . and advise you." This seemed like God's promise that He would show him what to do. All Barnardo wanted was some sign from God to be sure.

A week later it came. A letter arrived from a complete stranger, Samuel Smith, M.P. He had heard of Barnardo's work and wanted to help. If Barnardo agreed to stay on in London and continue his work among the children, Smith would give one thousand pounds. Barnardo kept the letter secret for ten days so he could think about the offer.

For a little while now he had been thinking of opening a home for some of his boys. He felt that all the good work done by his mission would come to nothing, if afterwards the boys had to go back to the streets. They needed a home where they could receive loving care and attention. With this money he could start a boys' home.

He wrote to Samuel Smith, accepting his offer. He gave up the idea of going to China and made plans to open a boys' home. The year was 1870.

Boys' Home

Barnardo rented a large house in Stepney: Number 18 Stepney Causeway. He set about making the place fit to live in. Walls were knocked down to make five bedrooms. Bathrooms, lavatories, a kitchen and a wash-house were added. Later, when the Home was enlarged, a chapel and a library were built on.

The floors were scrubbed, and the ceilings and walls whitewashed. Rooms were prepared for a "father" and a "mother" who were to care for the boys.

When everything was ready, Barnardo spent two nights searching for boys who were willing to enter his Home. He had no problems in finding enough boys, though there were always some who wanted to keep their freedom. He took in boys and not girls for a special reason. He was still only aged twenty-five and unmarried, and felt that he could deal with boys better than girls.

At first he chose only twenty-five boys, although the Home was able to take sixty. He did not have enough money left to take care of more, and he did not want to get into debt. This meant that for a while he had to turn some boys away.

One eleven-year-old boy nicknamed "Carrots" was very sad when there was no room left for him. He pleaded with Barnardo to take him in. He had lived on the streets since he was seven, he said. He had no father, and his mother had turned him out of the house. It was weeks since he had eaten a proper meal.

It was difficult for Barnardo to refuse, but he had made up his mind. He gave the boy some money with which to buy food, and told him that he could have the first place that became free.

But that was never to be. A few days later some market porters moved a barrel. They found two boys inside who appeared to be asleep. One of them jumped up and ran away, but the other did not move. He was dead, killed by cold and hunger. It was Carrots.

13

When Barnardo heard of the boy's death, he was stunned. He blamed himself for what had happened. He decided that no other child should suffer in this way, if he could help it.

He put up a large notice outside the Home. It said that no child without a home would ever be turned away. In future

The Home in Stepney Causeway

14

he would never turn away a homeless child, even if it meant getting into debt. From then on he kept every bed filled.

Young man with a lantern

Sometimes boys came to the Home and asked to be taken in. More often it was Barnardo who found the boys and invited them in.

He used to go around the East End three nights a week, searching for boys sleeping out. He carried a lantern so that he could look into the dark corners and other hiding-places where boys usually crawled for the night. He left at about midnight and got back at five or six in the morning.

Each time he moved to a different area. One night he would try the Thames barges. On another night he would go to Billingsgate Market or to Covent Garden. He visited fairs, factories and public houses.

His pockets were always filled with pennies and pieces of cake, to win the boys' friendship. For those who refused the offer of a house, he had cards with his name and address printed on them. Many boys who turned down his first offer, had second thoughts and came to ask for a bed.

Soon the name Barnardo became even more well known in the East End of London. People began to trust him and turn to him for help. Everybody thought well of "the Doctor", as they called him. (This was despite the fact that he still had not passed his exams at the hospital.)

One night a gang of boys attacked Barnardo as he was searching the slums for homeless boys. They knocked him down and stole his money, his watch and chain, and even his hat and overcoat.

An hour later they caught up with him again. They had realised who he was and wanted to return his things.

"If we 'ad known it was you, sir, we would never 'ave done it," they confessed. "Sorry about it, sir".

Twelve months after Barnardo opened his Boys' Home an important law was passed in Parliament. It said that in future all children between the ages of six and ten must go to school. School board officers were chosen. It was their job to see that children went to school, instead of working in a factory or walking the streets.

As a result, some boys were now more ready to accept Barnardo's offer of a home. It was better to go to his school than attend day school.

Boys learning a trade

Training the boys

Barnardo ran his Boys' Home in a very strict way. Every boy had to get up at six o'clock each morning, and be in bed by ten o'clock at night. They had to make their own beds, scrub the floors and wash their own clothes.

Every morning, except Sundays, the boys had school lessons. They spent every afternoon in the workshops learning a trade such as carpentry, shoemaking and printing. Some boys were apprenticed out to various tradesmen. When they left the Home, usually about the age of sixteen, they were able to get a job and earn their own living.

Barnardo also realised the need for healthy bodies. The boys had regular P.E. lessons, and there was a large yard where they could play football. Then, in their spare time, some of the boys had music lessons and were able to form a brass band. The band often played at Barnardo's meetings.

Each day at the Home began with prayers. Every week the boys had religious education lessons. On Sundays they all went to morning service. Being a Christian had made a big difference to Barnardo's life, so he wanted to share his faith with his children. As a result, many of these young lives were deeply touched by what they saw and heard.

Home for Girls

There were homeless girls as well as boys on the streets of London. So far, Barnardo had not felt able to help the girls, though he had often worried about them.

Three years after opening the Boys' Home Barnardo got married. Like her husband, Mrs Barnardo had also run a school for poor children, and she shared her husband's faith and ideals. Perhaps they could now take in homeless girls?

They already had a suitable building close to their home.

All that was needed was some furniture and household equipment. Mrs Barnardo took charge of the work and made all the arrangements.

At first only twelve girls were taken into the Home. They were difficult girls, and came from very unhappy homes. Nearly all of them had a record of crime. Over the next year the number of girls rose to sixty. Some of them were found jobs as cooks or as servants in large houses. All seemed to be going well with the new Home.

And yet Barnardo was not happy with the girls' progress. There did not seem to be the change in the girls' lives that he had hoped for.

Thinking about the problem one night, he had an idea. The girls should not be housed in one large building like the boys; they needed to be in a family, like ordinary girls. He decided that he would build a village of cottages, where the girls could live in small groups, looked after by a "mother". In that way, the girls would have more care and attention.

Some weeks later, as he travelled to Oxford by train, he talked to a friend about his plan. What did he think about it? The friend replied that they should pray and ask God what He wanted Barnardo to do. The two men knelt down in the train and prayed. Next morning their prayer was answered.

While Barnardo was getting ready for breakfast at the hotel there was a knock at the door of his room. He opened the door.

"Is your name Barnardo?" asked a stranger.

"Yes."

"I hear you are thinking of building a village for girls and that you want some cottages?" the man went on.

"Yes, that's true."

"Have you got any yet?"

"Well . . . no, not yet."

"Then I'll buy the first one for you," promised the man. At that he left.

It turned out that this man's daughter had died recently. He and his wife wanted to do something as a result of which her name would be remembered. The man had heard of Barnardo's plan and felt that this was just the thing.

When the news got out, other people soon began to offer to pay for a cottage. Before long there were enough offers to enable Barnardo to start building the village. Three years later the Village Home for Girls was opened at Barkingside, Ilford, in Essex. It consisted of twenty-five cottages.

With a family

As time went on, Barnardo found that there were more and more children in need of his help. Ten years after he opened his first Home, he had 1000 children in his care. By the time of his death the number had risen to 8000.

After a while, Barnardo was forced to enlarge the Home in Stepney Causeway. Later he opened a second Home in London, called Leopold House. Other Homes were opened in places like Birmingham, Cardiff, Leeds, Liverpool and Newcastle.

Any child was accepted, regardless of age, sex or religion. The greater the need, the greater the welcome.

Once again Barnardo began to realise that he ought to care for his children in a different kind of way. He saw that the boys would be better off living in a family group rather like the girls in his Village Home. Perhaps they could be placed in *real* families, where they would have brothers and sisters?

As the thought grew in his mind he decided to put it

19

into action. To find the right kind of families for his plan, he asked supporters of the Homes to help him. Instead of choosing the families himself, Barnardo asked his friends to suggest suitable homes to him. He especially wanted homes where the children would be made welcome and loved.

These new parents were known as "foster parents". They were not the children's real parents, but people who acted as mothers and fathers to the children until they were old enough to look after themselves. When the time came, the children could return to Barnardo's to train for a job before going out to earn a living.

The plan was a success. In the first year 330 boys between the ages of five and nine were boarded out in 120 families. Next he placed some of his girls, and then babies, with families. By the time of his death, twenty years later, he had placed over 4000 children in good homes.

Special care

Barnardo showed special interest in children who were either very ill or handicapped: blind, deaf, dumb or crippled children. Some were like this because they had been born handicapped, or suffered from some disease. Others had been badly beaten and injured by their parents, or had not been given enough food.

To begin with, he opened a small hospital across the road from the Stepney Home. Here he was able to visit the patients and even to be present when any of them had to have an operation.

On one occasion he was talking to a lady visitor when he had an urgent message. He turned to the lady.

"Excuse me," he said, "but I must leave you. I have just heard that one of my boys is dying. He wants me to sit with him and hold his hand."

As far as possible Barnardo placed his handicapped children with the healthy ones. In this way the healthy ones learned to care for the others.

But there were some children who needed very special care. For these he opened a Home for cripples at Ilford, called Children's Fold. A few years later further Homes were opened in Lancashire and Yorkshire for children with incurable diseases.

Now Barnardo was able to look after children of all ages and conditions. Yet his work was not yet finished and he still had two great plans to put into action. When it became difficult for him to find good jobs for some of his boys, he sent them to Canada, where they could begin a new life. And before he died he was able to see another of his dreams come true. He founded a training-ship, in which many of his boys were taught to be sailors.

Money

As the number of children in his care increased, more money was needed to pay for their keep. It cost £15 a year to keep a child. Then there were other expenses, like rents and building repairs. For several years his helpers received no wages but only their board and lodging.

How did all this money come in? As Barnardo put it, mostly "by prayer and appeal".

In the early days money came in because the older boys did jobs to earn their keep. Barnardo formed a "City Messenger's Brigade", for which some of the boys took messages for shops and business firms. He also had a "Wood Chopping Brigade" and a workshop where boys made boots and shoes to sell. By these means the boys raised nearly £2000 a year for the Homes.

When people saw the good work being done by Barnardo, they began to send money. Some gifts were small, others large. A lady came to Barnardo's office one day and laid three £1000 banknotes on the table.

"I bring you this," she said, "because your door is never closed to any poor child. God will surely help you."

The woman refused to give her name, and no one knows to this day who she was.

Whatever he did, Barnardo always prayed first. He found that God answered prayer, and his children never went without the things they needed.

One winter, for example, he realised that he needed extra blankets. He learned that the cost would be £100. He was sure that God would provide the money, so he placed the order. Two days later he received a letter and a cheque for that amount. The writer said that he felt the boys would need "more warm clothing during the cold weather".

During the course of his life Barnardo received over £3¼ million for the work of his Homes. Yet despite his efforts to avoid getting into debt, he died owing nearly £250 000. However, a fund set up in memory of Barnardo soon cleared the debt.

The man himself

Barnardo was a small man, smaller than some of the boys in his Homes. But he was always smartly dressed, and took great care over everything that he did.

He had a great love of children, and they found him easy to get on with. The children enjoyed it when he came to read stories to them. He often played with his children, and his pockets were filled with sweets when he visited them. He was especially tender towards handicapped children, and spent a lot of time making sure they were well looked after.

When the children grew up and left Barnardo's, he kept in touch with many of them. He asked them to write to him, to tell him how they were getting on. Every year, about the time of his birthday, he held a big party for them. He talked to each one of them, asked how they were and gave them his advice if they had a problem.

He was a hard worker, sometimes spending as much as sixteen hours a day at his office. In one month, for example, he received 27 390 letters and, with the help of his staff, replied to nearly all of them!

Although Barnardo had a large number of workers, he liked to pick most of them himself. He took an interest in all that they did. They were very loyal to him, even though he was not an easy man to work with. He could be stern and cross with his staff, but he was also kind and thoughtful. In turn they admired his courage and discipline, and the way in which he cared for them.

Although he suffered a number of illnesses, he kept on working as long as he could. In the end, however, the strain of running the Children's Homes began to tell on him.

When he died, someone said of him, "Earth is poorer, Heaven is richer."

BIOGRAPHICAL NOTES

Thomas John Barnardo was born in July 1845, in Dublin. Although regularly taken to church by his parents, at the age of sixteen he confessed to being agnostic. Soon after, however, he was converted to Christianity, and he spent his spare time teaching in a Ragged School and visiting the homes of poor people. In February 1866 he heard the missionary Hudson Taylor speak about his work in China. To Barnardo this was his call from God – he believed God wanted him to be a missionary too. In preparation for this work, he moved to London to train as a doctor. Some key dates are:

1866 Opened his Ragged School in the donkey stable.
1868 Founded the East End Juvenile Mission.
1870 Opened the Stepney Boys' Home.
1873 Married Syrie Elmslie. Opened a Home for Girls at Mossford Lodge.
1876 Qualified as a surgeon. Village Home for Girls opened.
1882 First Barnardo boys sailed for Canada.
1886 Boarding-out scheme started.
1903 The Watts' Naval Training School established.
1905 Died, aged sixty years.

There were also other Christians working in London at the same time as Barnardo, to help people who were poor or homeless. William Booth, founder of the Salvation Army, started his Christian Mission in 1865; Dr Stephenson opened a Children's Home in South London in 1869; Edward Rudolf founded the Church of England Children's Society in 1881; and Benjamin Waugh founded the N.S.P.C.C. in 1889.

THINGS TO DO

A Test yourself

Here are some short questions. See if you can remember the answers from what you have read. Then write them down in a few words.

1 Where did Barnardo hold his Ragged School?
2 Why did Jim Jarvis want to stay by the school stove one night?
3 Why did poor people often turn their children out of home?
4 Where was Barnardo's first Children's Home?
5 Why did Barnardo at first take no more than twenty-five boys into his Home?
6 What happened to "Carrots" after Barnardo was unable to give him a place?
7 What was the notice Barnardo put up outside his Boys' Home?
8 Who helped him start the Home for Girls?
9 How did some of his boys help to raise money for the Home?
10 How much money did Barnardo receive for his Homes during his lifetime?

B Think through

These questions need longer answers. Think about them, then try to write two or three sentences in answer to each one. You may look up the story again to help you.

1 Why were Ragged Schools needed, and what sort of things were taught there?
2 How did Barnardo go about finding boys to offer them a place in his Home?
3 In what ways did Barnardo feel that God spoke to him and guided him?
4 Why did Barnardo think it was better to place some of his children with a real family rather than place them in a Home?
5 Describe one time when Barnardo said he had an answer to prayer.

C To talk about

Here are some questions for you to talk about with each other. Try to give reasons for what you say or think. Try to find all the different opinions which people have about each question.

25

1 Why are some parents cruel to their children? What should be done about it?
2 Do people get real answers to prayer? Or is it just coincidence?
3 Do you think handicapped children should go to ordinary schools? Could healthy children do anything to help them?
4 Why do you think Barnardo was so successful at raising money for his Homes? Did his faith in God have anything to do with it?

D Find out

Choose one or two of the subjects below and find out all you can about them. History books, geography books and encyclopaedias may be useful. Perhaps you can also use reference books in your library to look up some of the names and places.

1 *Dr Barnardo's Homes*
    (a) Try to find out more about Barnardo by reading some other books.
    (b) How many Homes and Centres are run by Dr Barnardo's today? In what different ways does Dr Barnardo's care for children?
    (c) Find out your nearest Dr Barnardo's Home and try to arrange a visit there. Afterwards write a report showing how the children are looked after.

2 *Other Children's Homes*
    (a) Find out about the National Children's Homes and the Church of England Children's Society. How were they started, and where? What do they do to help children today?
    (b) What other children's Homes can you find out about?

3 *National Society for the Prevention of Cruelty to Children*
    (a) Find out about Benjamin Waugh's work in Greenwich, London, and that of T. F. Agnew and Samuel Smith, M.P., in Liverpool.
    (b) How did the N.S.P.C.C. start? What was the Children's Charter?
    (c) What kind of work does the N.S.P.C.C. do today?

4 *The Welfare State*
    In Barnardo's time, anyone who did not have enough money to live received no help from the State. The only place where they could go was the workhouse.
    (a) What was a workhouse, and what did the people do there?
    (b) What is meant by the term "Welfare State"?
    (c) In what different ways does the State help people in need today?

USEFUL INFORMATION

Addresses

Dr Barnardo's
Tanner's Lane
Barkingside
Ilford
Essex IG6 1QG.

National Children's Home
85 Highbury Park
N5 1UD.

Church of England Children's Society
Old Town Hall
Kennington Road
London SE11 4QD.

National Society for the
Prevention of Cruelty
to Children
1 Riding House Street
London W1P 8AA.

N.B. Remember to enclose a stamped, addressed envelope for the reply.
A postal order for 50p would also be helpful, if you want plenty of material.

More books to read

Ever Open Door, by Carolyn Scott (Lutterworth) (P).
Father of Nobody's Children, by Norman Wymer (Arrow Books). Available
    from Dr Barnardo's (P/T).
The Story of the Children's Home, by Alan Jacka. Available from the
    National Children's Home (T).
The Welfare State, by R. Cootes (Longman) (P).

(T) = suitable for teachers and older pupils
(P) = suitable for younger pupils

Films

Dr Barnardo's – The Changing Need (19 min), colour. This and other titles
    available from Dr Barnardo's.
The Goal of the League (18 min), colour. This and other titles available
    from the National Society for the Prevention of Cruelty to Children.
Kaleidoscope of Care (30 min), colour. This and other titles available from
    the National Children's Home.

Filmstrip

Victorian Social Life: The Life of the Poor, colour. Available from Longman Group, Pinnacles, Harlow, Essex CM19 5YA.

Slides

Life in Victorian England: Town Life, The Poor (S478), colour, tape or cassette commentary. Available from The Slide Centre, 143 Chatham Road, London SW11 6SR.

Pack

Social Problems: Secondary History Pack (Longman).